A DARK SHAPE

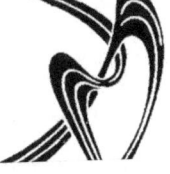

INTERRUPTED THE LIGHT THAT PRESSED IN FROM THE OUTSIDE WORLD.

JANUS TURNED AND SAW THE DARK FORM BLOCKING THE EXIT. HE FELL BACK AGAINST THE WALL, HIS BREATH GONE.

JANUARY

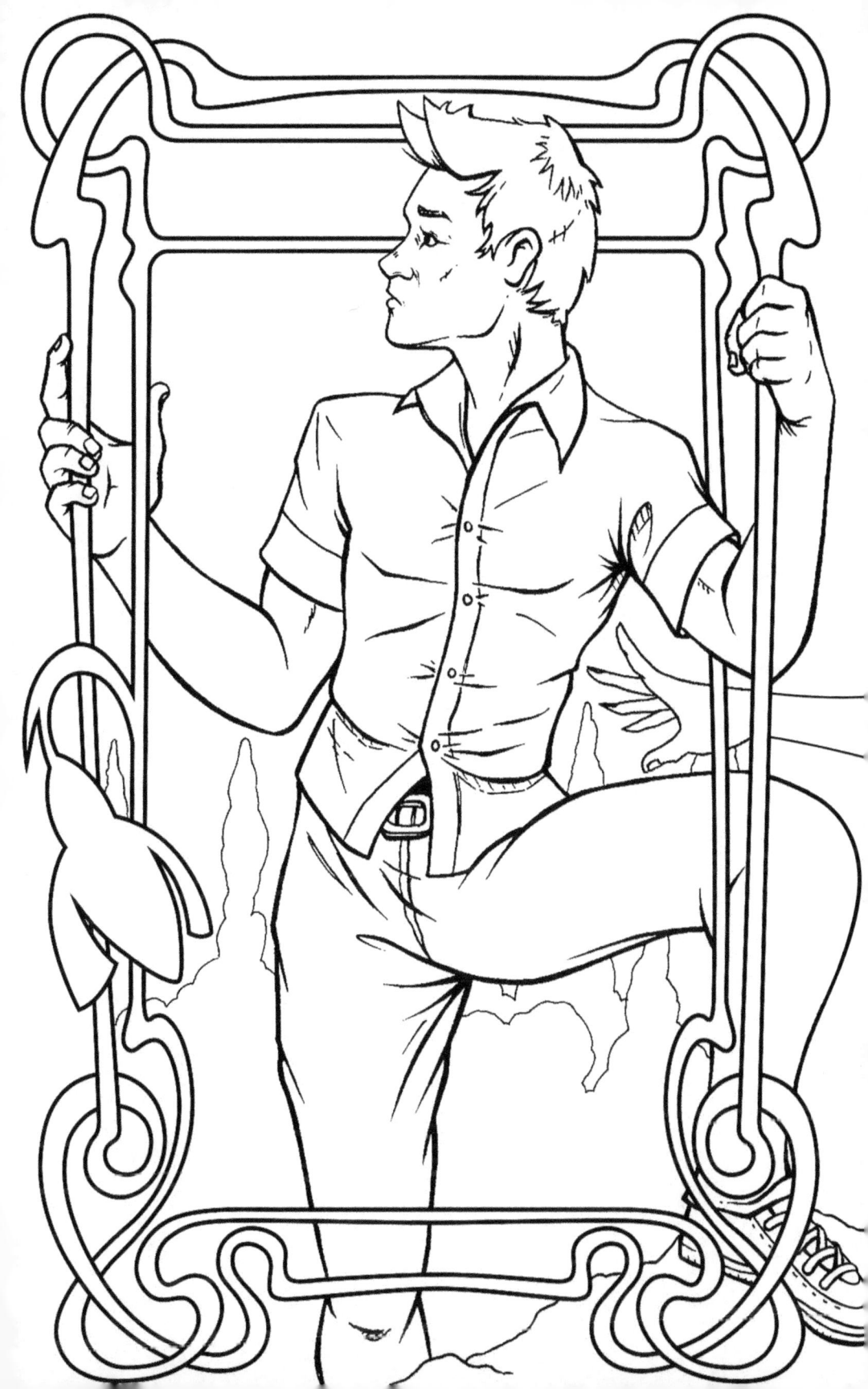

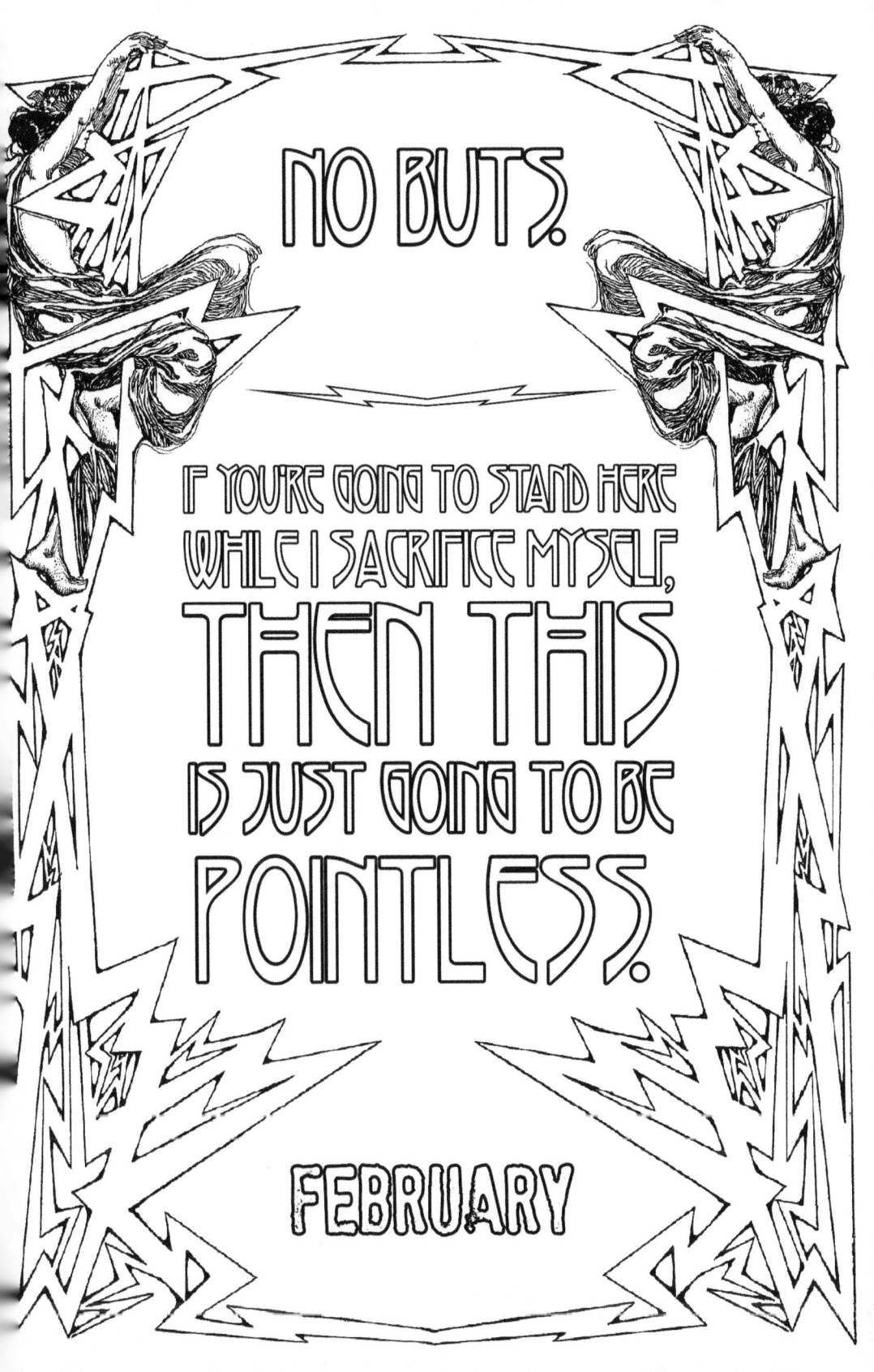

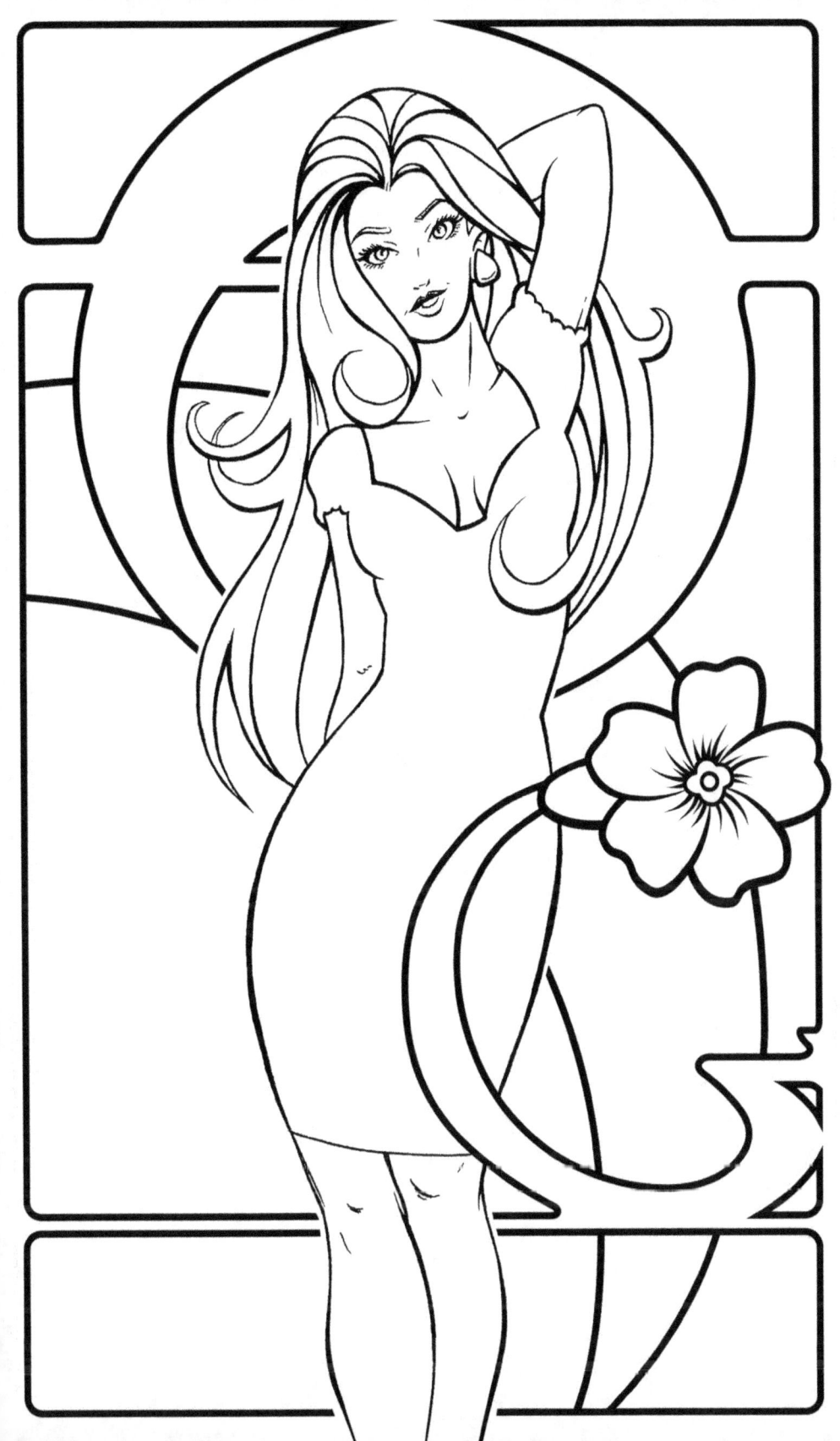

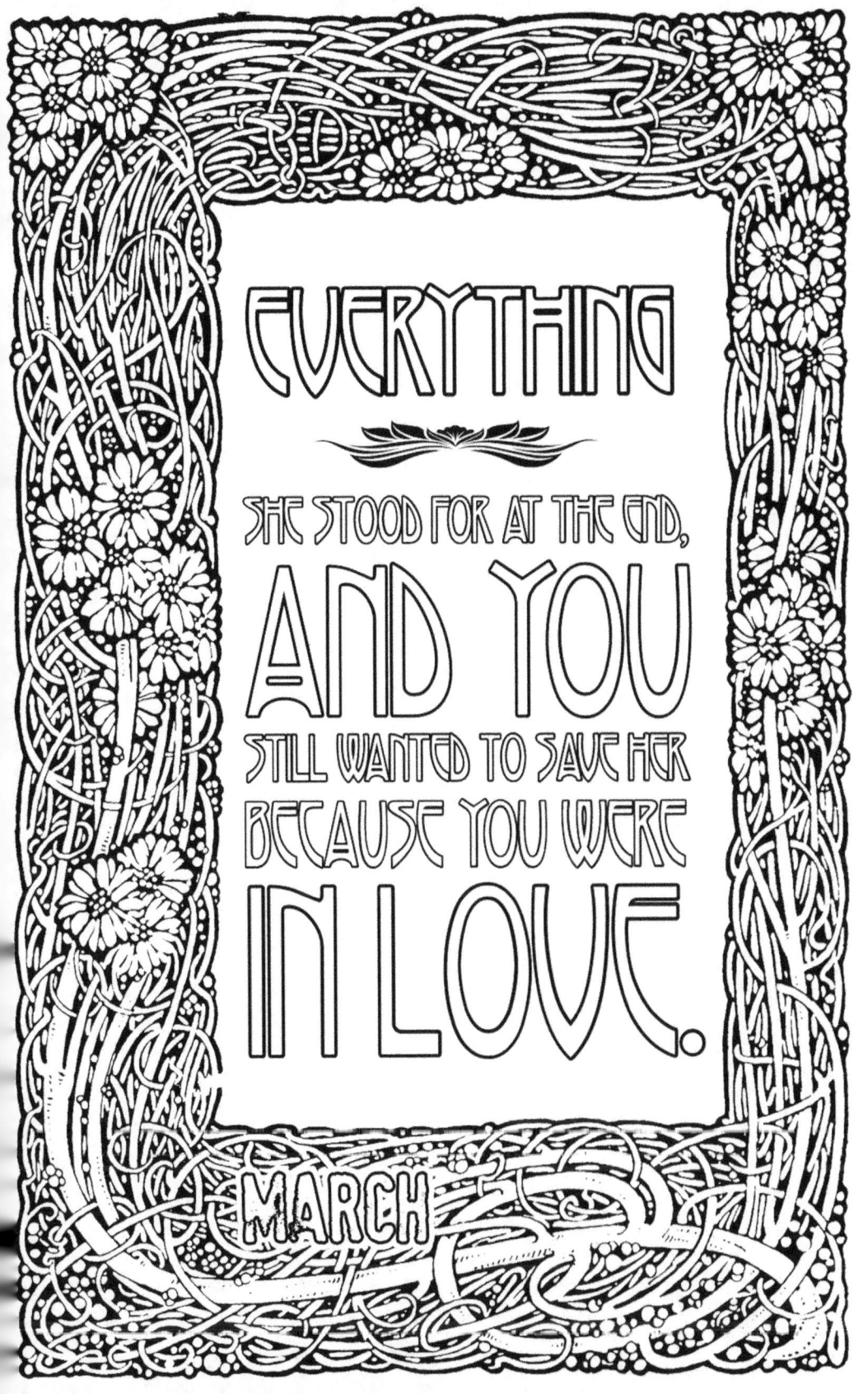

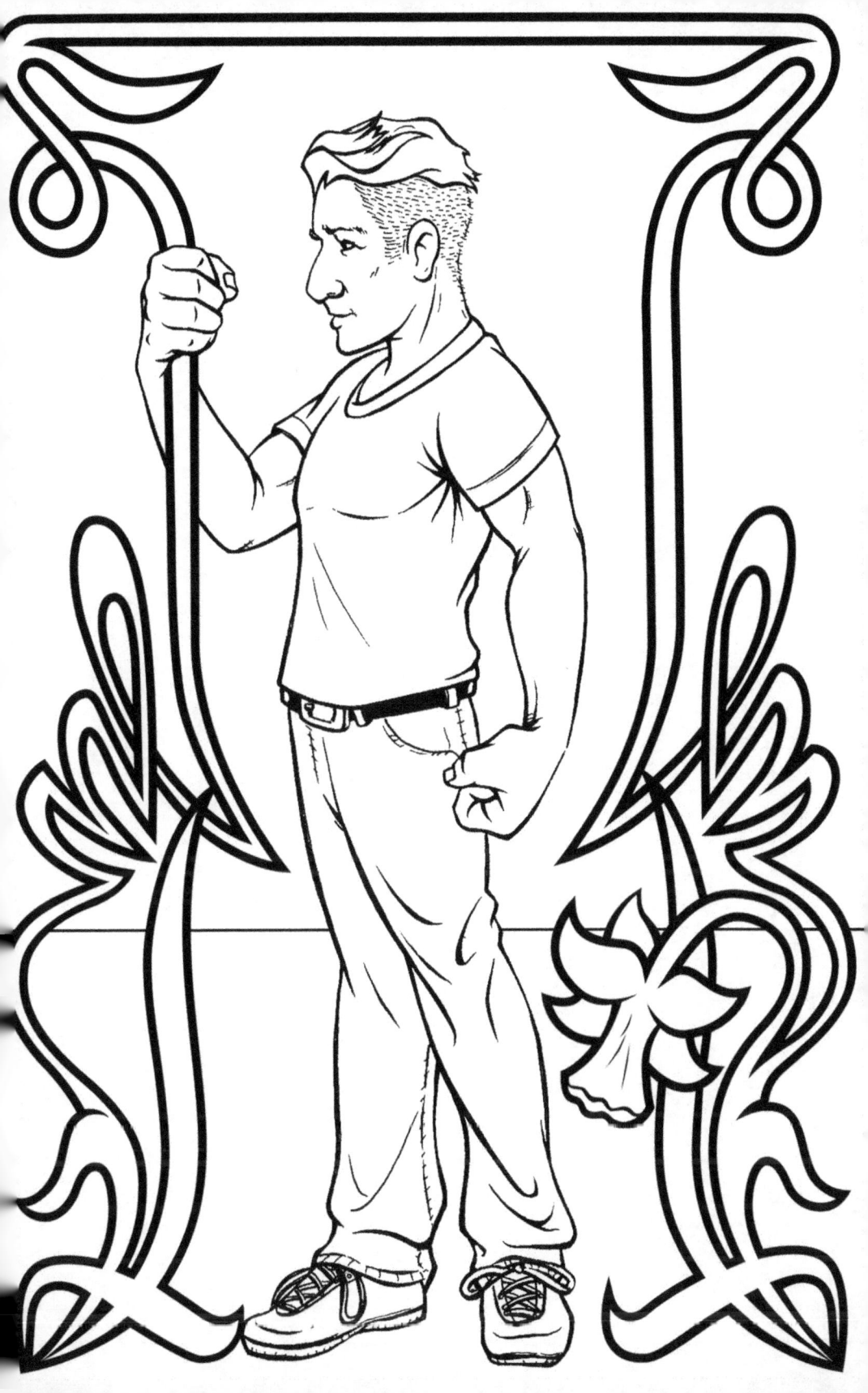

SHE'S BITTER, AND SHE'S WICKED.

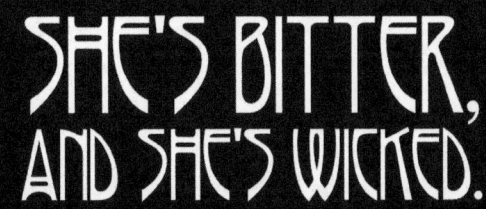

SHE'S GOING TO LIVE UP TO HER PROMISES.

APRIL

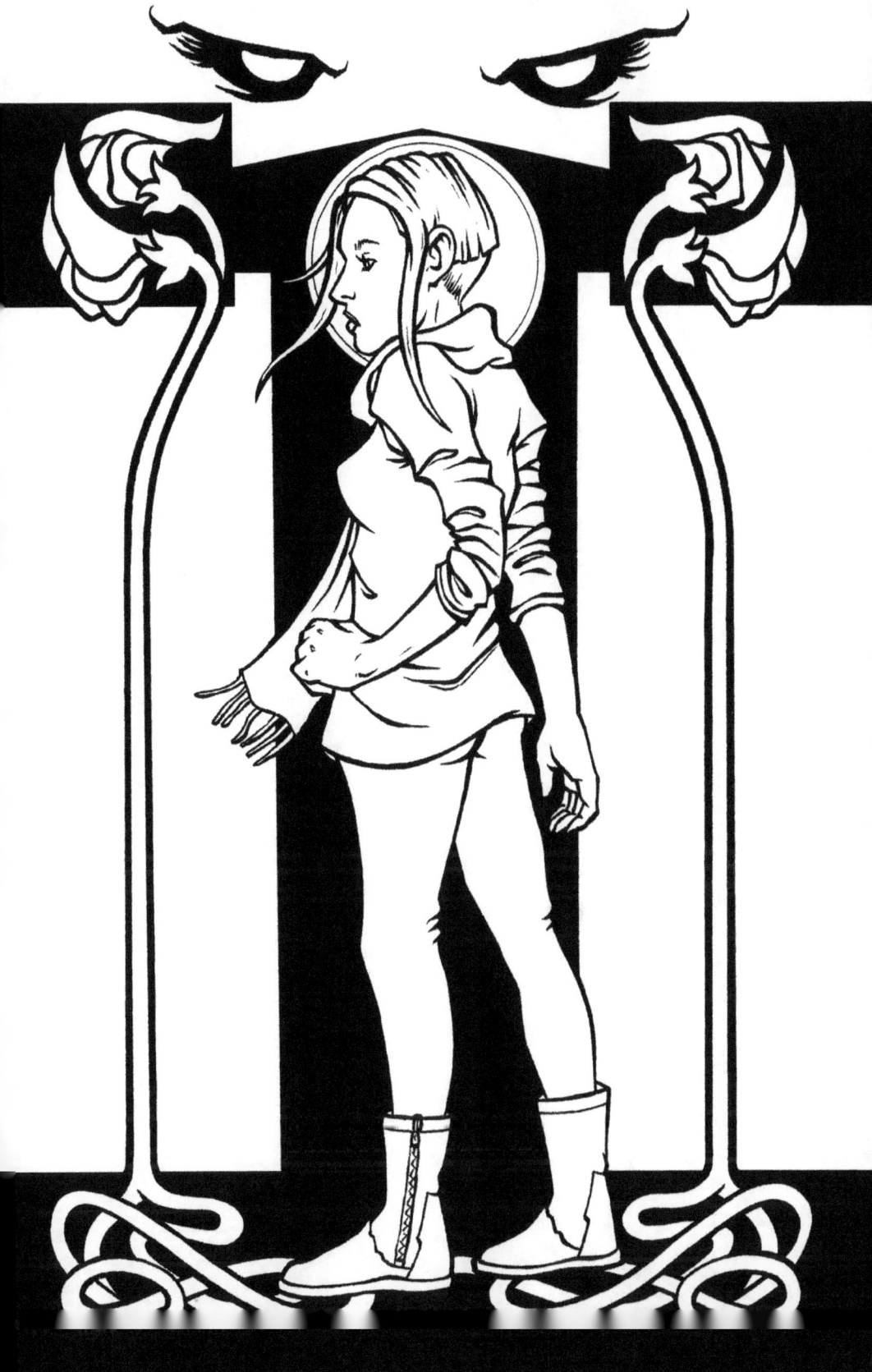

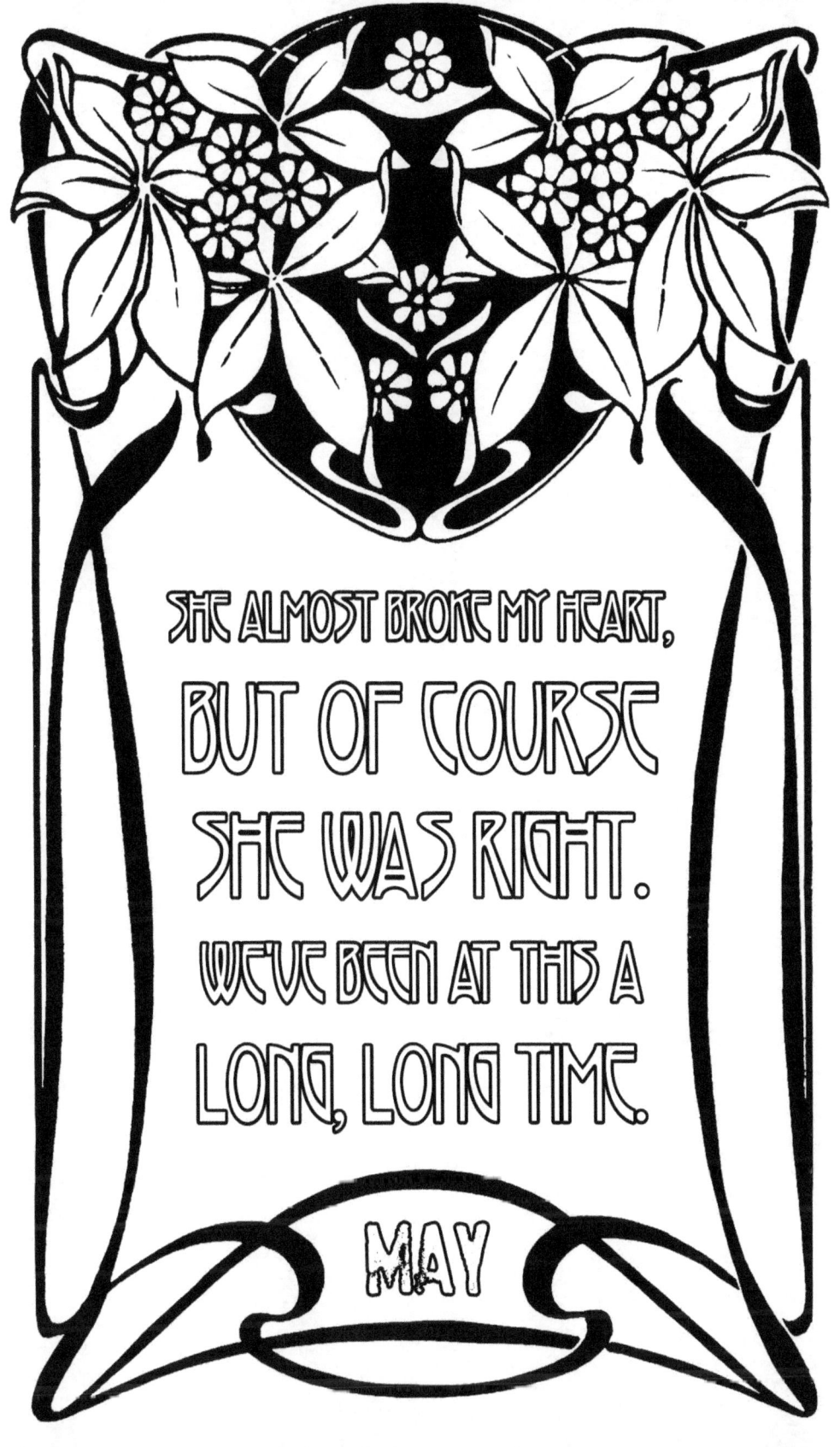

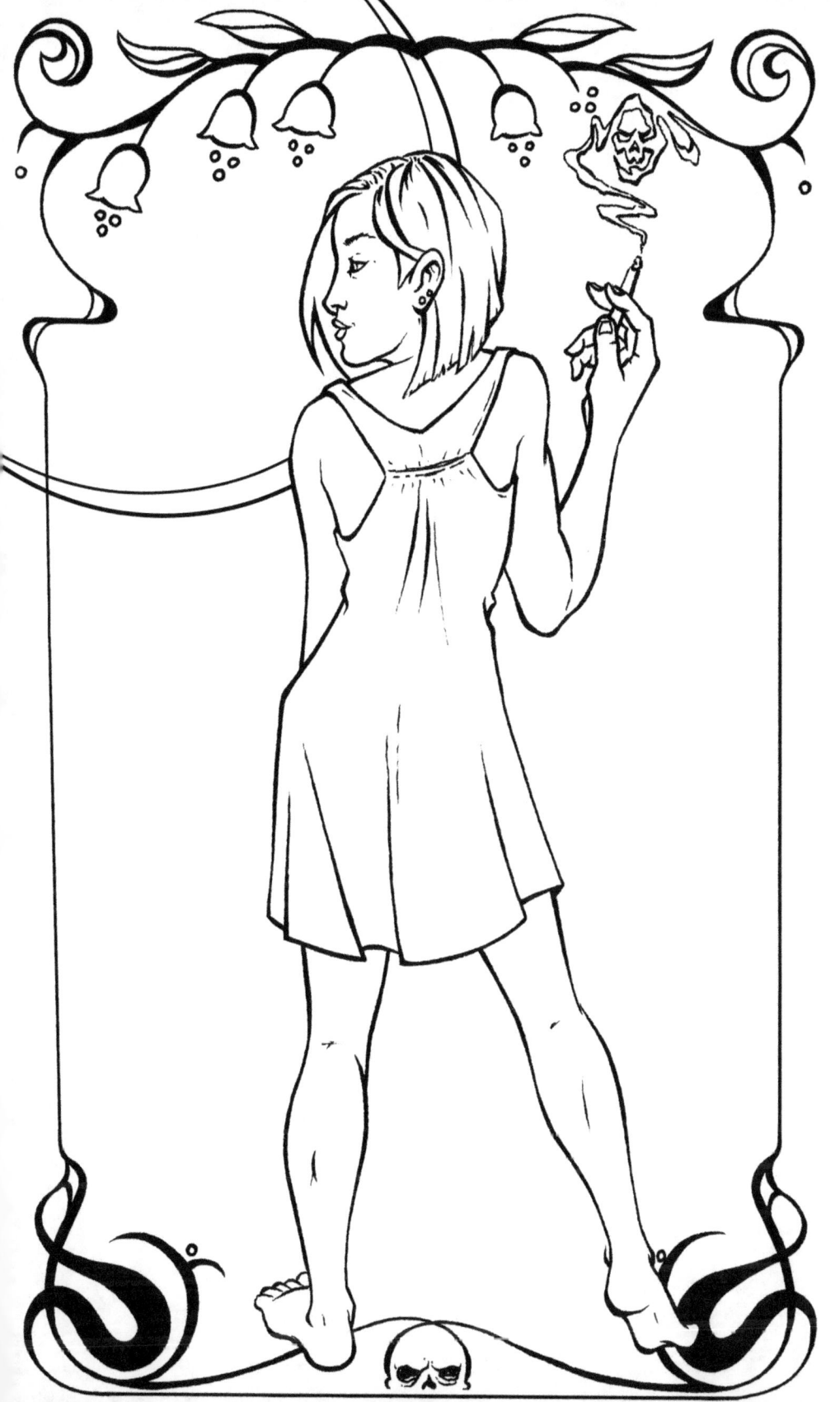

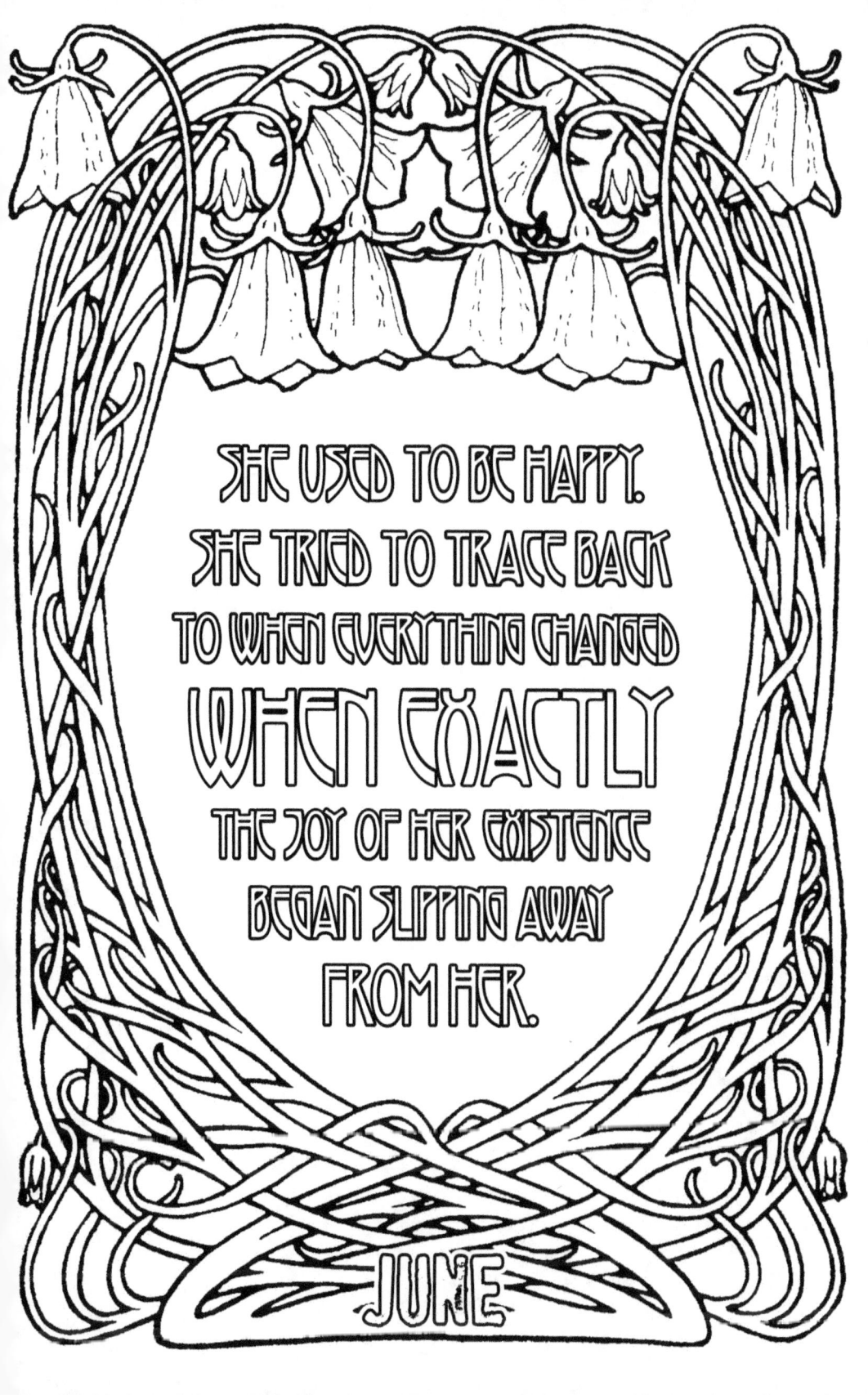

SHE USED TO BE HAPPY.
SHE TRIED TO TRACE BACK
TO WHEN EVERYTHING CHANGED
WHEN EXACTLY
THE JOY OF HER EXISTENCE
BEGAN SLIPPING AWAY
FROM HER.

JUNE

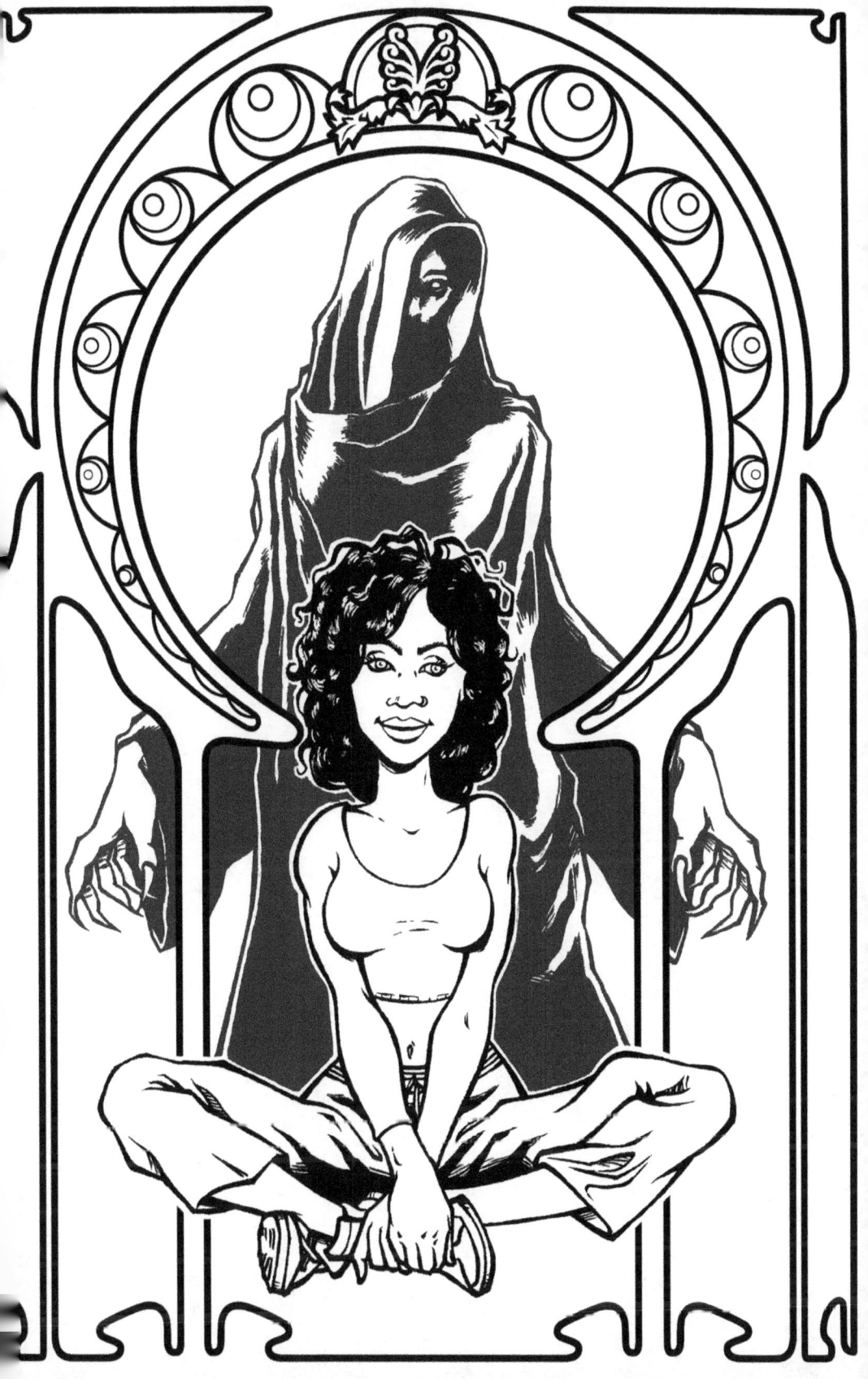

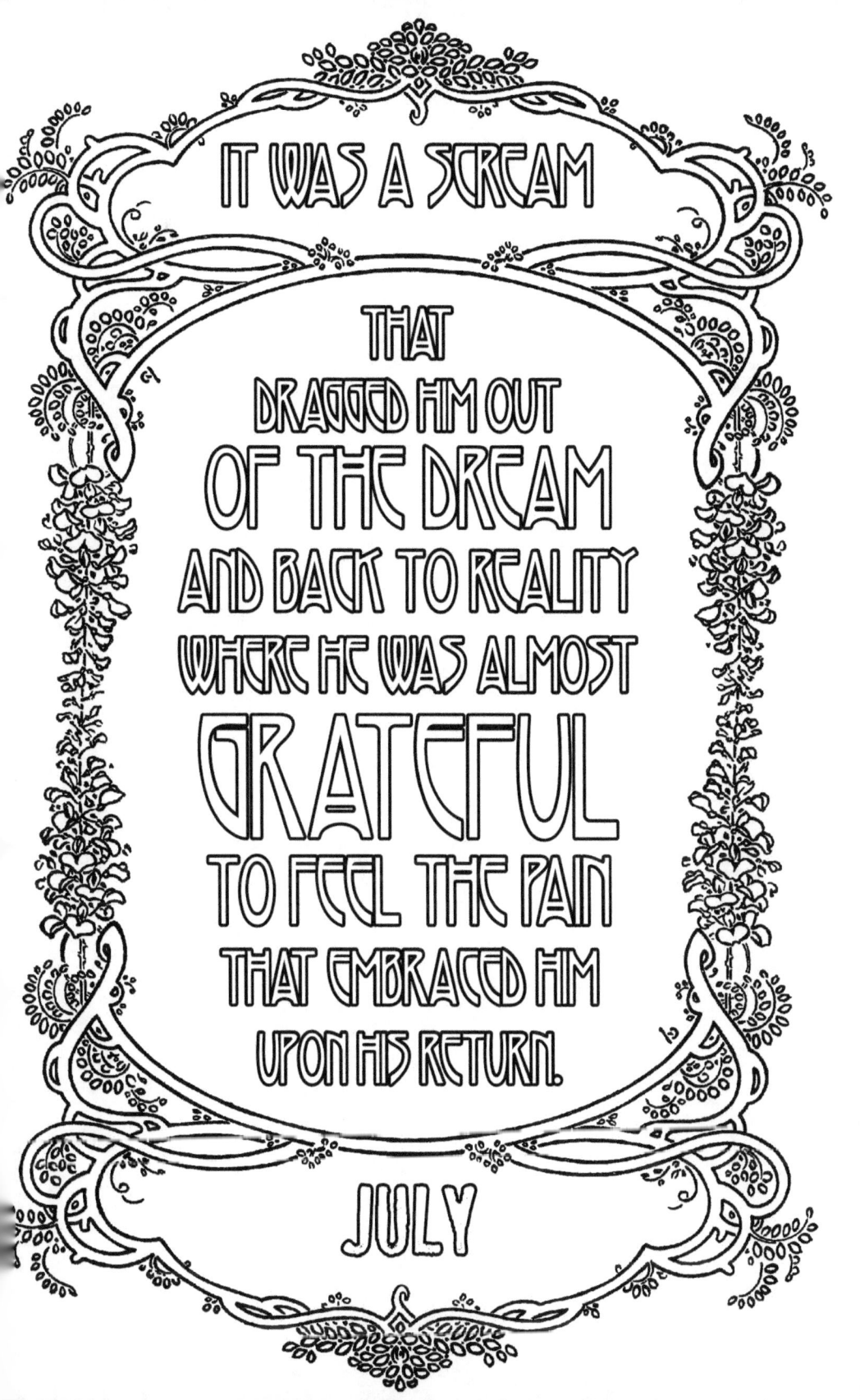

IT WAS A SCREAM

THAT
DRAGGED HIM OUT
OF THE DREAM
AND BACK TO REALITY
WHERE HE WAS ALMOST
GRATEFUL
TO FEEL THE PAIN
THAT EMBRACED HIM
UPON HIS RETURN.

JULY

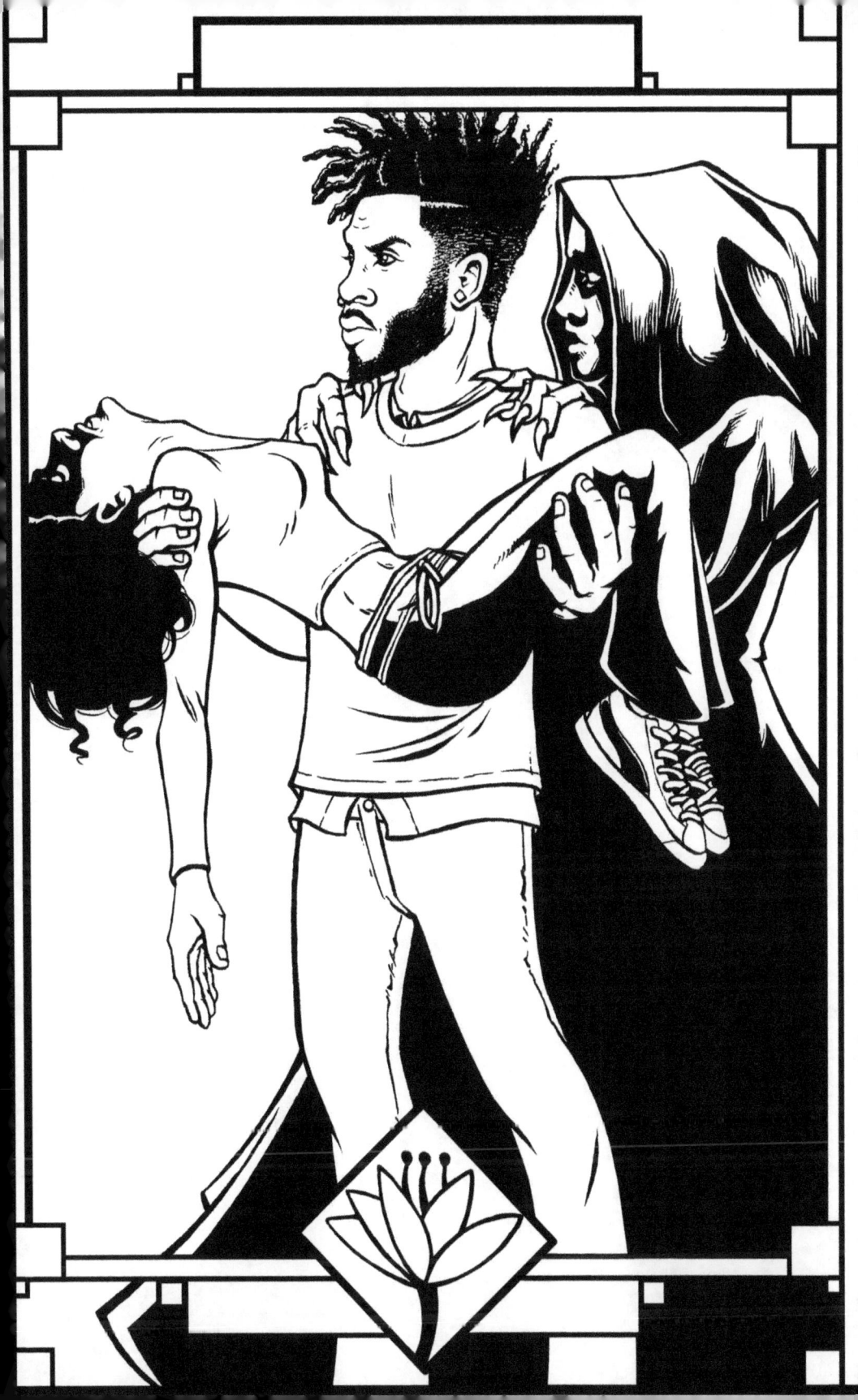

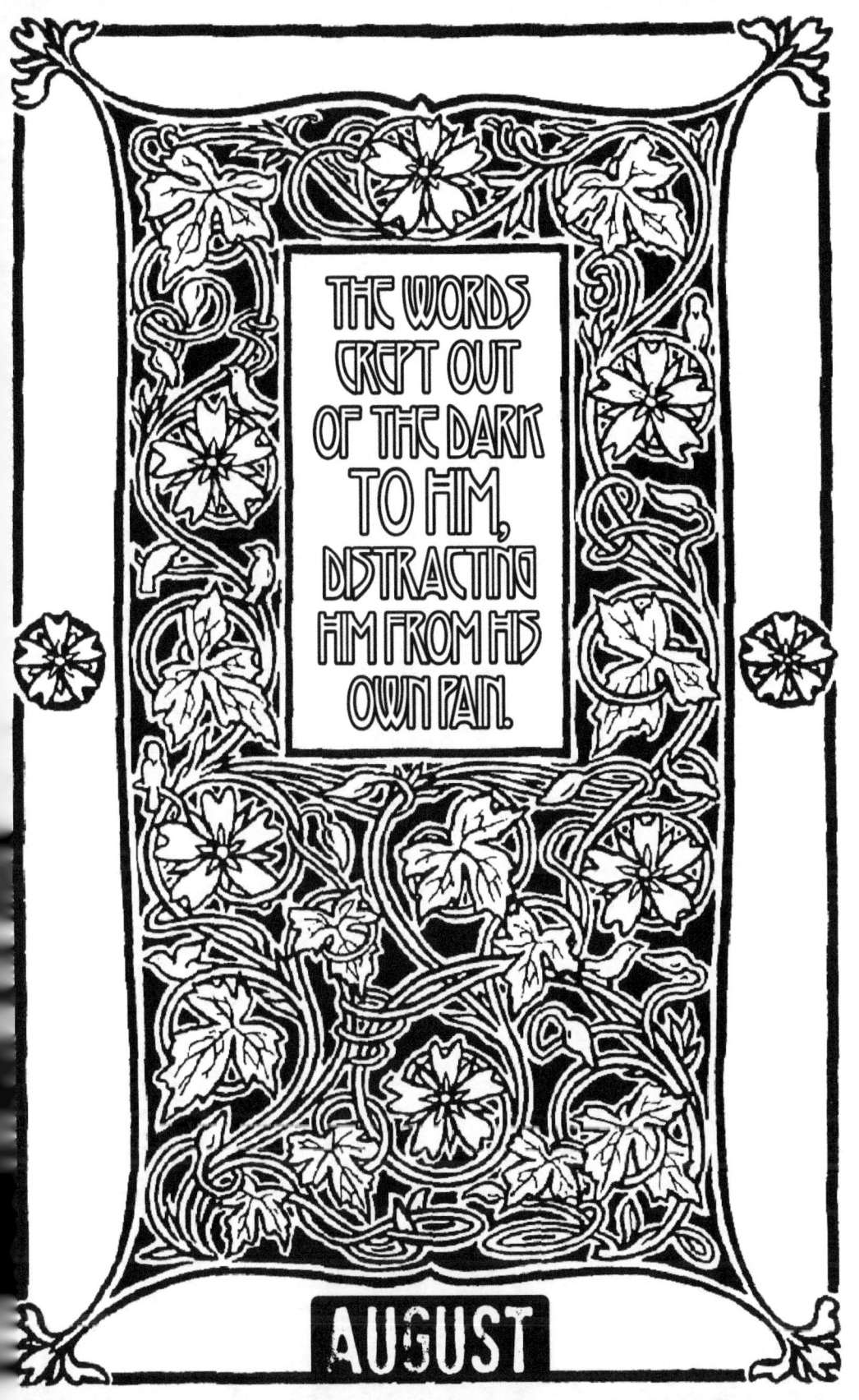

THE WORDS CREPT OUT OF THE DARK TO HIM, DISTRACTING HIM FROM HIS OWN PAIN.

AUGUST

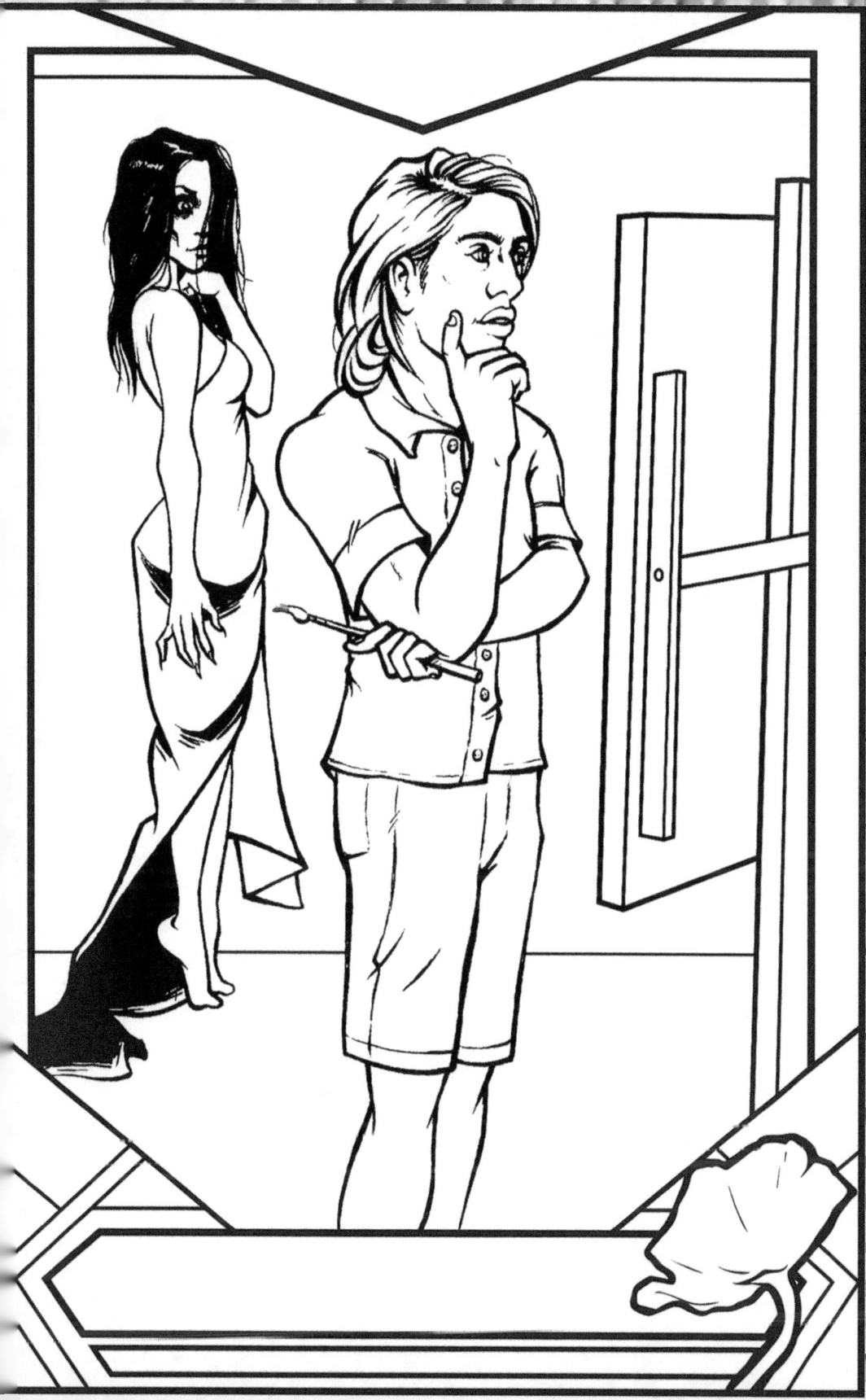

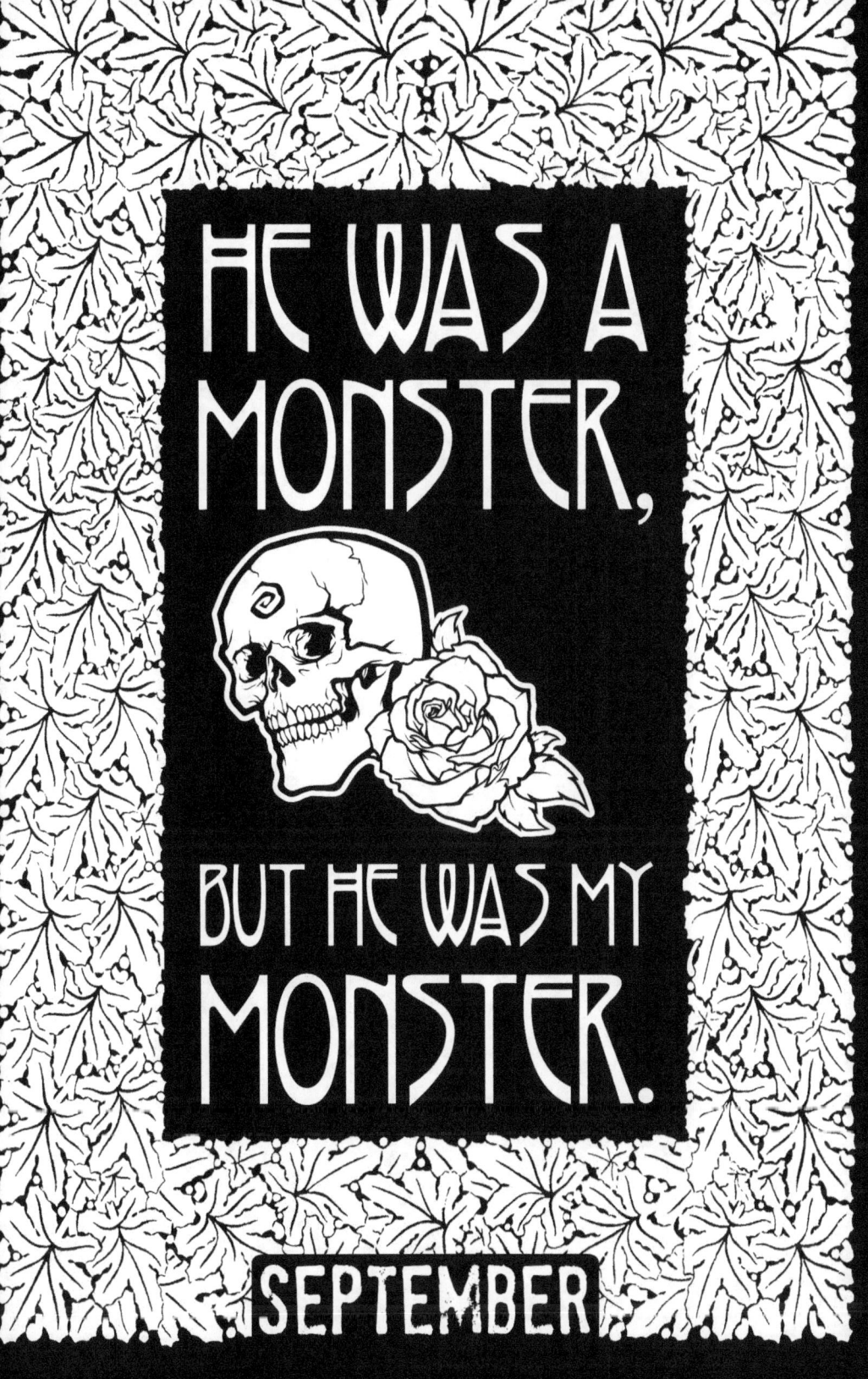

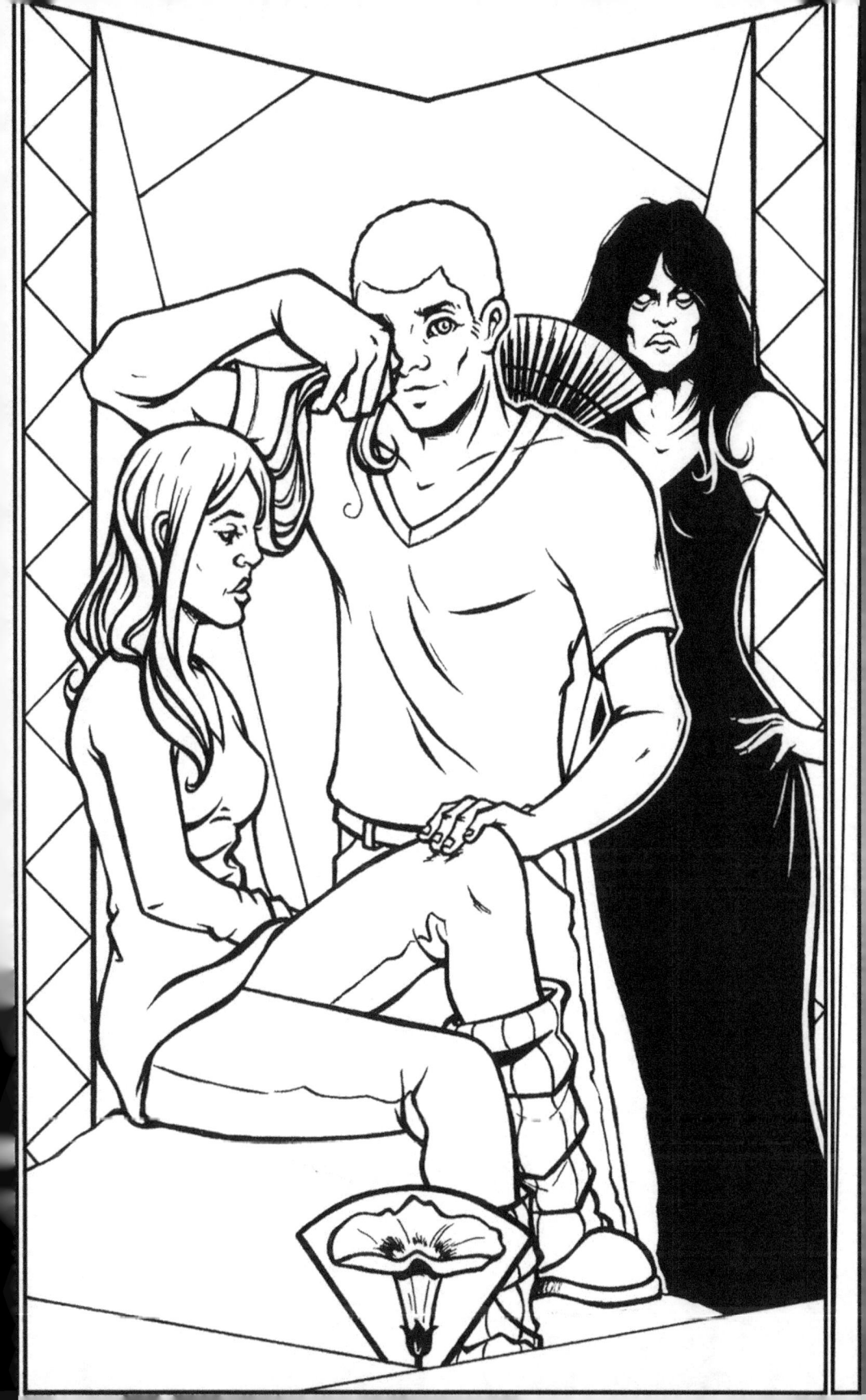

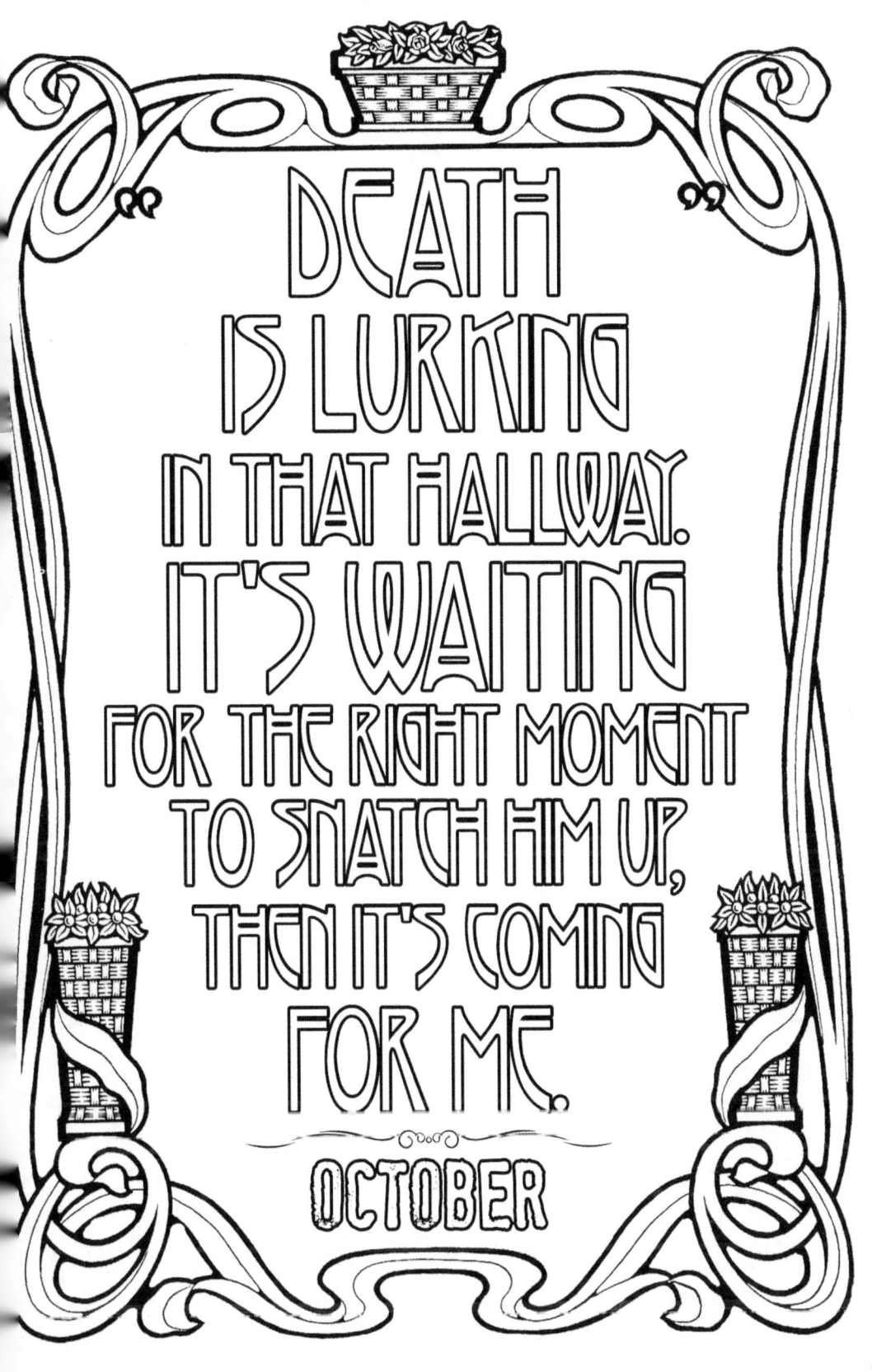

DEATH IS LURKING IN THAT HALLWAY. IT'S WAITING FOR THE RIGHT MOMENT TO SNATCH HIM UP, THEN IT'S COMING FOR ME.

OCTOBER

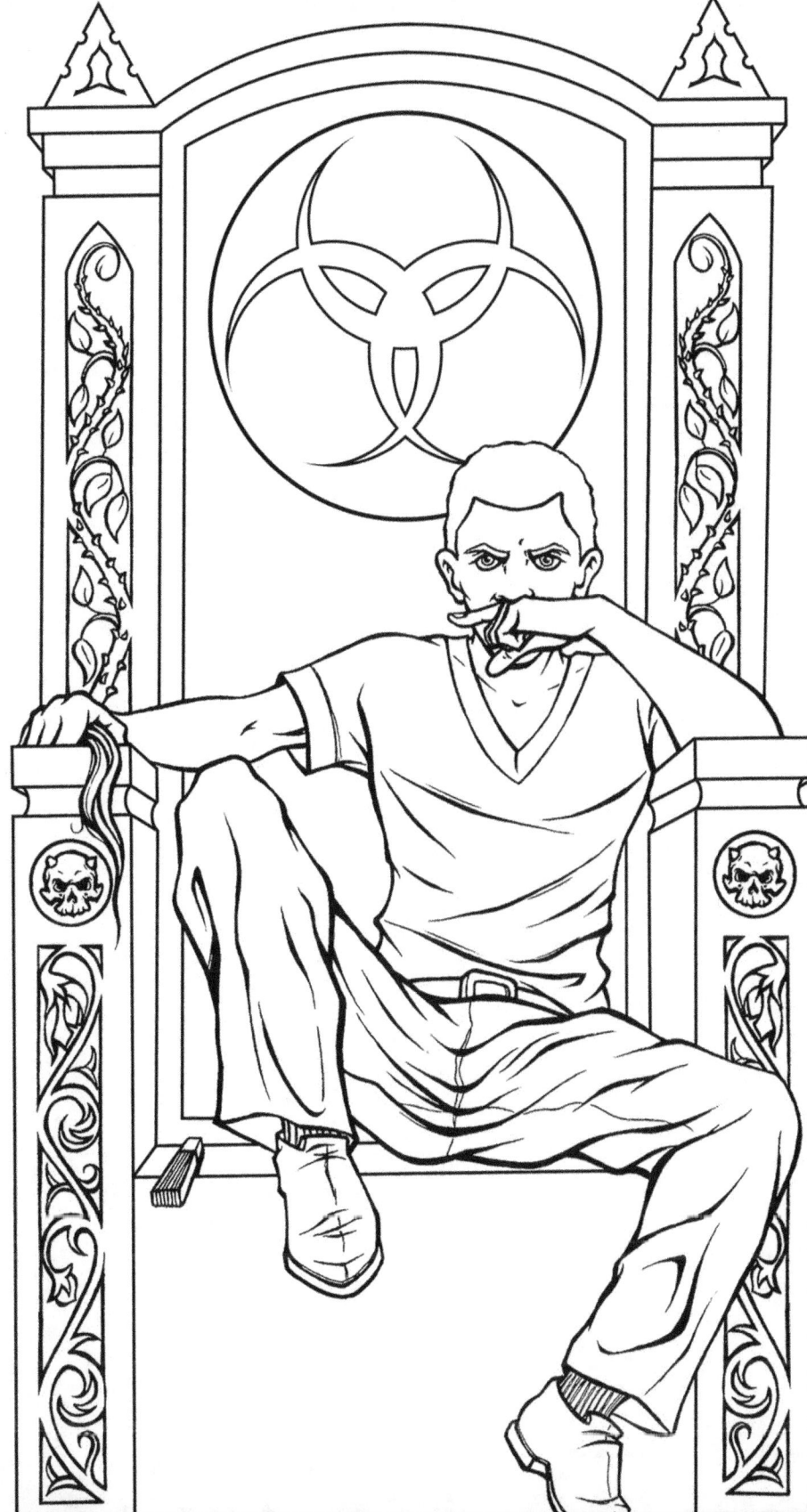

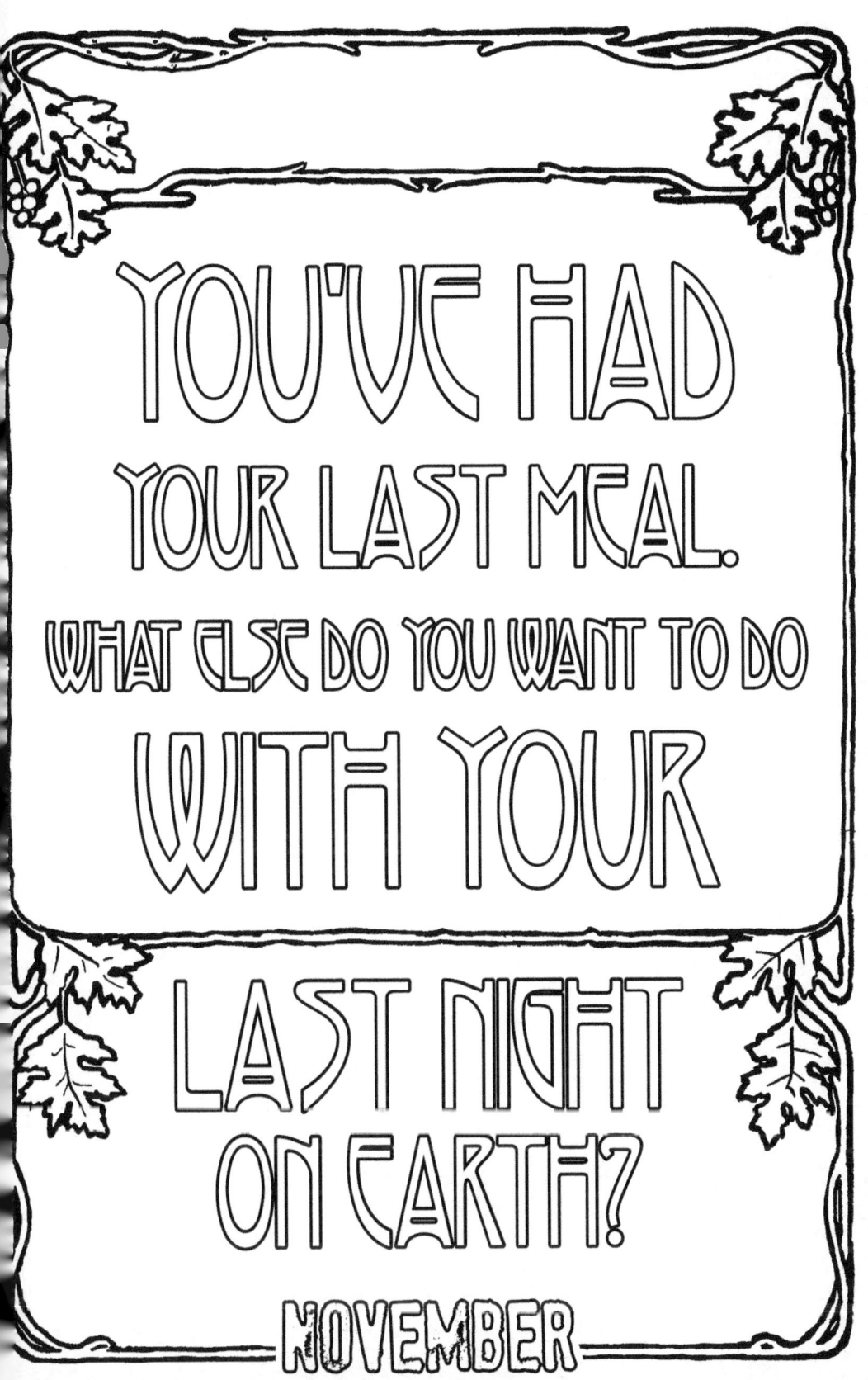

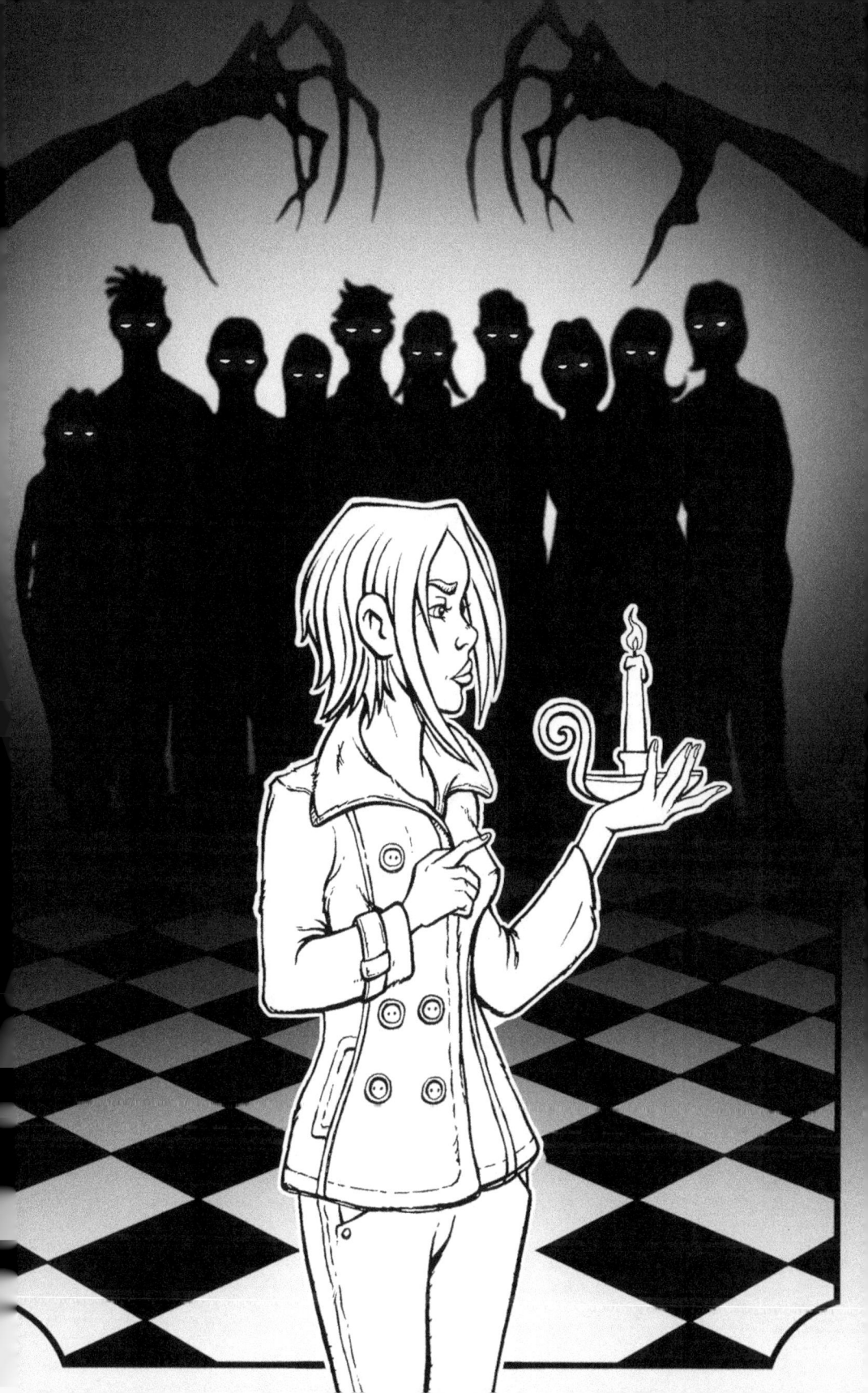

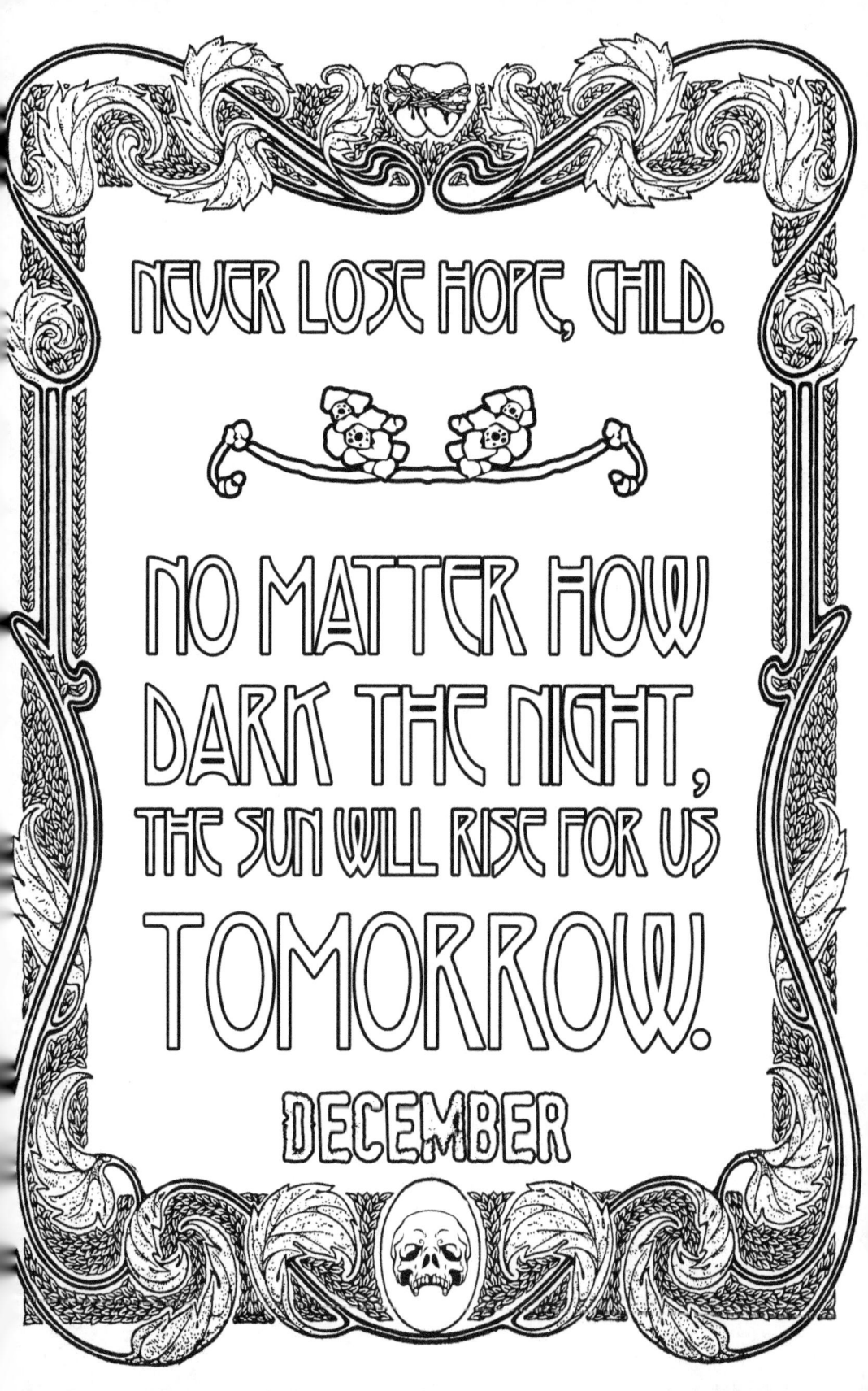

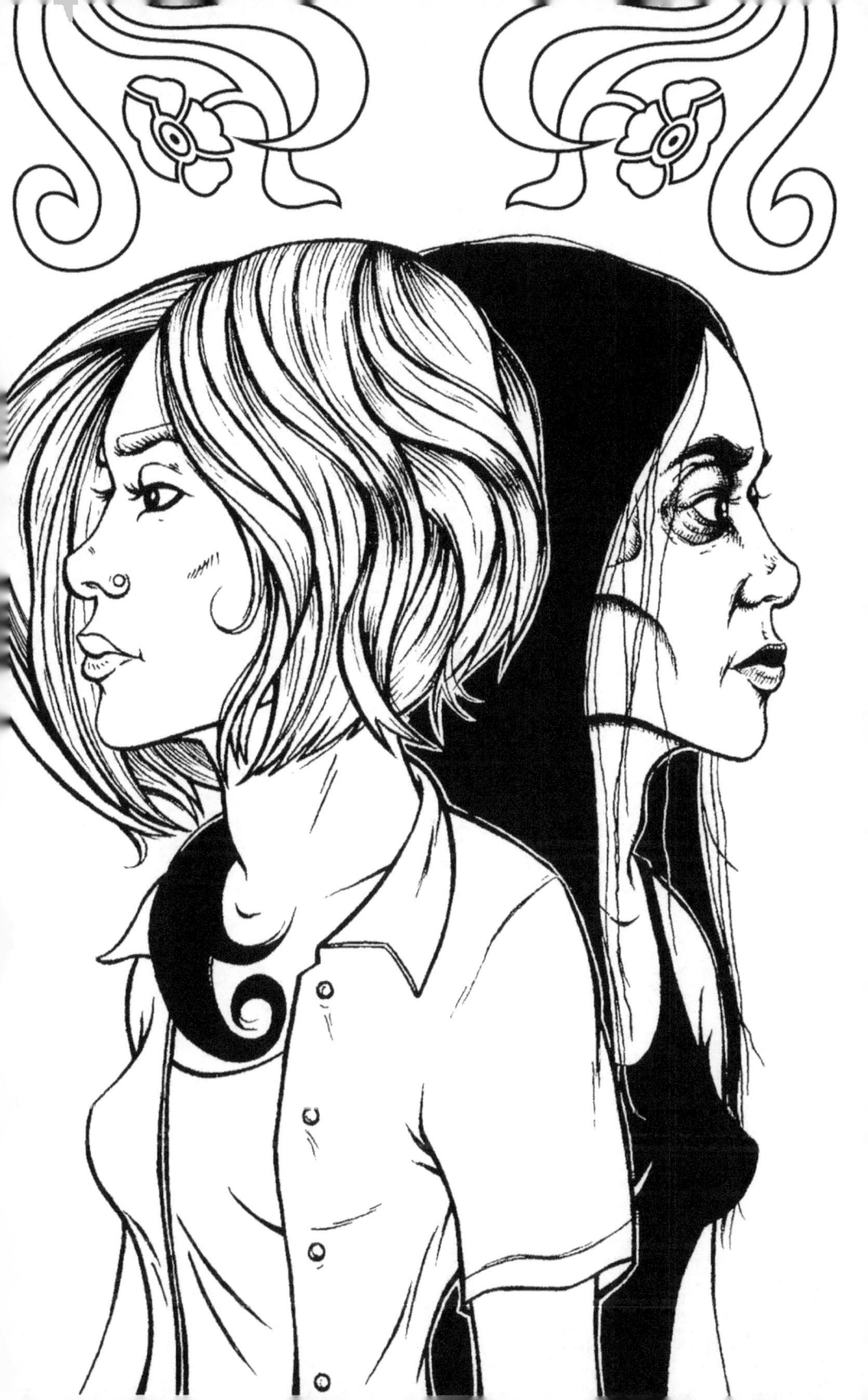